CW00838895

The road from fat to thin doesn't have to be paved with frustration, sacrifice, and hunger. On the contrary, it can be a path of pleasure, increased energy and "joie de vivre". Food and drink aren't just a source of calories – they provide us with the fuel we need to sustain feelings of wellbeing, happiness, and a healthy, beautiful body.

We know from experience that dieting makes us gain weight. No wonder, since there are really only two activities that are truly effective: to lose weight we have to eat and exercise. Our bodies need all the nutrients in nature. If we miss out on even one, we slow down the wheel of life and lower our metabolism. In this book, you'll learn how to eat fat burners instead of fat storers. In other words, you'll discover how to eat the foods that make you thin and give you energy. Why wait? Open up this book, and learn how to fill your tank with super fuel for greater zest and vitality.

Super Fuel: Fat Burners

The easy way to melt off pounds

We have to eat in order to lose weight. This simple truth always elicits a certain amount of scepticism. It's deeply engraved in our minds that we must avoid calories, refuse fatty foods, and banish evil carbohydrates! And it's because so many of us believe this that so many people in this country are overweight. But whether we follow the latest diet in Hollywood or the one practised at the office, nothing works in the long run. The bitter result is the "yo-yo effect". We've struggled tediously to starve off those last few pounds and have finally arrived at our ideal weight when suddenly the yo-yo hits the end of its string and jumps back up to the top, each time climbing a little higher. Sound familiar?

It's time to put a stop to it all! Change your life. Throw out all calorie-saving measures. You have to eat to lose weight. And you'll notice that when you fill up your tank with "super fuel", you will feel more energetic, alive, and joyful than you ever dreamed possible.

The following five principles will guide you on your journey:

1. Carbohydrates with a low-glycaemic index let you shed pounds.
2. Fat doesn't just turn to fat – you need some fat in your diet.

3. Protein melts away the body's extra padding.
4. Without vital nutrients, your metabolism grinds to a halt.
5. Without exercise, you can't even begin.

Metabolism – The Wheel of Life

Your body contains a natural wonder – your metabolism. Think of it as the wheel of life, or a complicated biological system that converts the food you eat to energy, body tissues, creative thoughts, and joyful feelings. You determine all that you are, the way you feel, and the amount of strength and joy you experience each day, by what you choose to eat. The only thing is, your system is millions of years old. Four million years ago, our first human ancestor's biological system was programmed to run on a naturally pure diet of lean meat, fruits, roots, vegetables, and grains. Our system has remained the same but the fuel has changed dramatically. Up to 75 per cent of what we eat is produced in a factory. Admittedly, being able to take our vegetables from the freezer saves us time and encourages good health. At the same time, however, we overload our bodies with substances that our genes don't recognize. There's no genetic program for metabolizing instant soups, ketchup, sweets, and the like. The body strives in vain to defend itself, contracting illnesses of civilization such as obesity, diabetes, gout, heart disease, chronic fatigue, depression, and cancer.

The Wrong Fuel

If we treated our cars in the same way that we treat our bodies, they would never even make it out of the garage. From morning till night we fill our tanks with the worst kind of fuel, even though we know this destroys the engine: fast food and chocolate, white flour and sugar, preservatives and dyes, artificial additives and contaminants – all of them unfamiliar to our metabolism. Larger amounts of these substances throw off the delicate balance of hormones in our bodies. As a result we become fat – and unhappy. But we can take precautionary measures by avoiding processed products. Excessive weight is our body's response to a lack of vital nutrients. Packaged foods often contain a hotch-potch of dead nutrients, supplemented with flavourings and a few token vitamins to promote sales.

How to Lose Weight

Give your body's 70 billion cells the vital nutrients, basic materials, and energy they need and they will thank you with a lively dance of hormones, a powerful immune system, firm muscles, nerves of steel, active organs, and an attractive figure. If you neglect even one nutrient, your body will respond with fatigue, bad moods, dull hair, and extra pounds. It is a lack of certain nutrients that makes you fat. It is nutrients that help burn off the fat. Nutrients are the fat burners.

Low-Glycaemic Carbohydrates

Warning – sugar is stronger than your will!

Carbohydrates come from such diverse sources as sugar and honey, chocolate, sweets, wholemeal bread, fruits, and vegetables. The difference between them is that some of these foods make us fatter, while others are true fat burners that melt off the pounds. It all depends on their glycaemic index.

The Glycaemic Index

The glycaemic index determines whether you will be fat or thin. The glycaemic index formula is simple: carbohydrates that raise your blood sugar (in other words, those that enter your bloodstream rapidly) have a glycaemic index of over 50, meaning that they have the potential to make you fat. These include sugar, sweetened drinks, white rice, white flour, chips, and many more processed products (see table on page 5). Low-glycaemic foods (those with an index of under 50) stabilize your blood sugar level and are genuine fat burners. These include the natural carbohydrates derived from fruits, vegetables, and wholegrain products.

The Power of Sugar

Whenever you eat, you trigger a dance of hormones in your body. These hormones control your energy metabolism. They either deposit the fat on your hips or take it and transport it to the mitochondria, tiny kilns in your cells that combust the fat into heat.

Glucagon, for example, is a fat-burning hormone. Insulin, on the other hand, is a fat storer. Whenever you eat a high-glycaemic food such as sweets, white flour, or white rice, the sugar molecules quickly pass from the intestines to the bloodstream. Your pancreas doesn't know what is happening, since refined food was only introduced 500 years ago, so it panics. It dispatches an army of insulin to halt the advancing sugar barrage. The insulin either diverts the sugar from the bloodstream to the muscles, or converts it to fat on your hips.

Your blood sugar drops dramatically and rapidly and your brain's sugar supply is depleted. If you have no more sugar in your blood, you lose the ability to concentrate and become distracted, nervous, and tired. Your brain soon responds with a ravenous craving for something sweet. And you give it what it wants because sugar is stronger than your will. If you start your day with sugar you won't be able to end it without sugar.

Insulin Weight Gain

Carbohydrate craving is a phenomenon that causes people to gain weight. Usually, quick carbohydrates are combined with fat, whether in chocolate bars or chips. The insulin created by eating these substances sends the fat straight to your fat cells where it gets locked away. As long as insulin dominates your blood, glucagon, the fat-burning hormone, doesn't have a chance. As soon as you change your diet to fat burners – foods with a low-glycaemic index – glucagon will take over and send the fat to your muscles to be combusted. As for high-glycaemic foods, enjoy them in moderation and try not to combine them with fat.

Fat Storers – High-Glycaemic Foods

Beverages: beer 110; soft drinks, colas, sweetened fruit juices 80–100

Sweeteners: honey 75; sugar 75; chocolate 70; jellies and jams 60

Bread: white sandwich bread 95; French bread 70; mixed-grain rye bread 65

Potatoes: Fried potatoes 95; mashed potatoes 90; chips 80; boiled potatoes 65

Fruits and vegetables: Carrots 85; sweetcorn 70; watermelon 70; pineapple 65; raisins 65; bananas 60; melon 60

Grain products: Cornflakes, popcorn 85; rice cakes, puffed rice 80; sweetened muesli 70; corn chips 75; crackers 75; croissants 70; wheat flour 70; white rice 70; couscous 60; pasta 60

Fat Burners – Low-Glycaemic Foods

Sweeteners: Unsweetened jam 30; fruit-flavoured ice cream (unsweetened, homemade) 35; unsweetened chocolate (over 70% cocoa) 20

Bread: Wholemeal bread 50; pumpernickel 40; whole rye bread 40

Fruits and vegetables: Fresh vegetables 15; mushrooms 15; fresh vegetable juices 15; fresh fruits 10–30; freshly squeezed fruit juices (unsweetened) 40; dried apricots 30

Legumes: soya beans 15; lentils 30; peas 50

Grain products: Whole-grain unsweetened muesli 40; oatmeal 40; rye 35; brown rice 50; whole-wheat pasta 30

Miscellaneous: Whole-milk dairy products approx. 35; low-fat milk 30; unsweetened natural yogurt 15; nuts 15–30

Fat Alone is not the Enemy

The right fats burn off unwanted padding

You need fat to burn fat. Even the most scorned fattener is actually a fat burner. Studies show that athletes who avoid all fat will suddenly gain weight while their muscles shrink. And no wonder! Essential fatty acids are as important as vitamins. Without them, your body is unable to produce fat-burning hormones. Fat isn't just your number one source of energy; it calms your nerves, builds your cells, makes your skin smooth and youthful, and cushions your organs and nerves – and without fat, you wouldn't be able to produce any hormones.

Eat Half the Fat – and Change the Type

Obviously you can't subvert the laws of conservation of energy. Energy doesn't just disappear. Whatever you put into your body and don't burn off in your muscles makes a stopover in your fat cells. Consuming about 60–70 g (2–3 oz) of fat per day will keep you lean and fit, provided it is not all saturated animal fats. Animal fats should be kept to a minimum; they are not fat burners. Instead make sure you consume unsaturated fatty acids. These are substances your body can't produce on its own. Good sources are vegetables, olives, nuts, seeds, and fish.

Fats That Keep You Thin

Your kitchen should always contain olive oil, the traditional oil of the slender centenarians living on the Isle of Crete. Olive oil supplies fatty acids that adjust the settings of your hormone balance to Lean, Fit, and Healthy. The same can be said of the omega-3 fatty acids found in fish. They control your body's super-hormones, the eicosanoids. If you eat ocean fish (such as herring, salmon, or mackerel) at least twice a week, you will stimulate a good number of these types of eicosanoids that will in turn give you better health, more vitality, a lighter mood, and protection for your heart.

Fat and High-Glycaemic Index

If you eat your pasta with a cream sauce or your roast beef with mashed potatoes, the potatoes and pasta (both have a high-glycaemic index) will increase the insulin in your blood, which will then immediately transport the fat in the beef or cream to your hips, and seal away the fat molecules inside the fat cells. This won't happen, however, if you eat your meat with whole-wheat pasta (low-glycaemic index). In this case the insulin is kept at bay, and the fat from the meat can be burned off in the muscle cells.

When planning you meals, remember the following:

- Avoid eating fatty foods with high-glycaemic foods (steak with chips, pasta with cream sauce, buttered bread with jam, pizza, chocolate croissants, white bread with cheese over 40 per cent fat).
- Create fat-burning combinations: Lamb with brown rice, turkey breast with boiled potatoes, chicken with vegetables, whole-wheat pasta with prawns, or wholemeal bread with tomatoes.

The Thin Commandments

- Use olive oil instead of animal fats. Use less butter, cream, and margarine.
- Practice "light" cooking: Brush oil onto non-stick pans for sautéing. Choose steaming and braising to preserve vitamins and your figure.
- Eat things with zero fat: Legumes, fruits, fresh fruits, and whole grains (rice, pasta, bread, muesli) contain little or no fat.
- Reduce your consumption of red meats and processed meats like sausage or bacon. Instead choose ocean fish, game, and poultry. Choose lean cuts of meat: fillets, escalopes, and loins.
- Always purchase low-fat dairy products and avoid prepared products, even if they say "light". Nature always does it better.

Power from Protein and Vital Nutrients

Make those pounds disappear as if by magic

Nature provides you with a miracle substance that takes off the pounds while you eat: protein. Protein does this for two reasons:
1. Your body devotes a great deal of its energy to converting dietary protein to valuable body materials such as muscles, hormones, your immune system, and materials for repairing cells, promoting youthfulness, and vitality. It does so by availing itself of stored fat. This makes protein a real fat burner.
2. Muscles and fat-burning hormones are made up of protein. If you don't consume 50–100 g (2–4 oz) of this high-power fuel every day you will lose valuable muscle mass, become sluggish, and consequently gain weight. But don't look to red meats and processed meats as your protein source. These foods supply purines, artery-damaging cholesterol, and saturated animal fats. Healthy sources of protein are fish, poultry, legumes, and low-fat dairy products.

Too Little Protein and Vital Nutrients Makes You Fat

Protein needs to be broken down in your stomach and intestines into its tiny building blocks, the amino acids. This is the only way this valuable material can be transported to the cells, fortify your immune system, and help build fat-burning hormones, muscles, nerves and organs. But if vital nutrients aren't present, the protein remains in your intestines without doing its job. It doesn't serve as a fat burner or high-power fuel for your body. As a result, many people suffer from a lack of protein.

Obesity is your body's response to too many "dead" nutrients and not enough vital nutrients. Vitamins and minerals act as the agents of energy metabolism. If they aren't present, fat can't be broken down and protein can't be utilized and converted to muscles and fat-burning hormones. In other words, you put on more and more weight.

The Six Rules of Slimness

1. Live naturally: Consume the fat burners available from nature. Every day eat five servings of fruits and vegetables. Snack on seeds and nuts, preferably raw. Reach for whole-grain and dairy products. Eat fish three to five times a week.

2. Get enough vitamin C: Ensure that you are getting enough vitamin C, which the body uses to break down fat. Citrus fruits are good sources, or opt for a supplement.

3. Consider a nutritional supplement: Due to modern methods of food production, little that is healthy remains in our foods. Fill up your empty tank with high-quality vitamin and mineral supplement. Be conscious of the vital nutrients that burn fat: calcium, magnesium, chromium, iodine, selenium, and B vitamins.

4. Eat fitness-promoting combinations: Always combine protein (dairy products, meat, and fish) with carbohydrates (vegetables, salad, and fruit). This will provide you with both the vitamins you need for protein metabolism and the sugar you need for your brain. It will force your body to use its cushion of fat, to convert the protein contained in foods into energy.

5. Stock up on protein: You need at least 0.4 g of protein per 1/2 kg (1 lb) of body-weight daily. If you eat one serving of protein every four hours, you will always have enough materials to produce the fat-burning hormones STH (growth hormone) and norepinephrine.

6. Never skip a meal: If you don't have time to make a full meal, mix up a protein shake. Look for prepared mixes at a healthfood shop. Instead of satisfying your hunger with an unhealthy sandwich, shake up a skinny drink and accompany it with fresh fruit.

LOW-FAT SOURCES OF PROTEIN

100 g (4 oz) contains	g of fat	100 g (4 oz) contains	g of fat
MILK & DAIRY PRODUCTS		**FISH**	
Buttermilk	0.5	Pike	0.9
Cheddar	32	Prawns	1.4
Cottage cheese	2.9	Rollmop herrings	16
Cream cheese, (low-fat)	0.3	Salmon	14
Edam	28	Trout	3
Feta	16		
Goat's cheese	21	**MEAT AND POULTRY**	
Milk, low-fat	2	Beef (fillet)	4
Mozzarella	16.1	Beef (roast)	5
Parmesan	25	Chicken	2
Probiotic yogurt	3.5	Corned beef	6
Yogurt, low-fat	0.1	Ham	3
		Poultry sausage	5
		Rabbit	3
FISH		Turkey breast	1
Cod	0.8	Veal (fillet)	1
Plaice	2	Venison	4
Lobster	1.9		
Mackerel, smoked	16	**MISCELLANEOUS**	
Mussels	1.3	Eggs	5.2
Oysters	1.2	Legumes, grains	Trace
Perch, sole, pollack	1	Tofu	5

Power Week

Lose up to 3.5 kg (7 lbs) in seven days with the glycaemic index formula

If you use the recipes in this book and follow the rules below, you can melt off 1/2 kg (1 lb) a day.

1. Exercise: Run or walk 30 minutes every morning on an empty stomach and at a moderate pace, with a fat-burning pulse of around 130. Keep track with a pulse monitor. Breathe in for four steps and out for four steps, breathing deeply and regularly. And if the pulse monitor alarm goes off, slow down until you feel like speeding up again. Run again in the evening.

2. Drink: Drink 3 litres (6 pints) of water with fresh lemon juice every day. Drinking a glass of water after dessert and before leaving the table aids digestion. Avoid all drinks containing sugar, as well as beer, which has a high glycaemic index. A single glass of dry white wine is fine.

3. Eat: Eat fat-burning combinations regularly. If you need to skip a meal, shake up a protein drink instead and eat some fresh fruit.

4. Pre-eat: Before every meal, eat a large bowl of salad. Feel free to take a larger portion of brown rice or whole-wheat pasta.

5. Train: Buy a latex exercise band with instructions. Exercise problem areas for 10–20 minutes, including your abdomen, hips, and bottom. Your body will then form fat-burning muscles and hormones.

6. Avoid the scales: Measure your progress by the fit of your jeans rather than by the scales. You're in the process of reducing fat and building muscles, which are heavier than fat.

7: Avoid sweets: Snack on unsweetened chocolate, which has a low-glycaemic index. A spoonful of fat-burning Three-Berry Jam will also do the trick (recipe on page 15). If you just can't stop thinking about chocolate, go running. The change of scene will redirect your thoughts.

And After the Fitness Week?

There is no "after". Run and eat your way to a new, thin, active life. Use sugar like a spice, and avoid white flour as much as possible. You don't have to practise total self-denial. It's a matter of what you do throughout the 365 days of the year. Just keep eating a lot of fat burners.

Power Week

Monday

- Apple and Raspberry Muesli with Yogurt ❋ Tomato Stuffed with Radish Yogurt
- Courgette Strips with Smoked Salmon
- Spaghetti with Herb Pesto

Tuesday

- Wholemeal Rolls with Tomato ❋ Strawberries with Two Dips
- Artichoke and Cherry Tomato Salad
- Monkfish Ragout with Lentils

Wednesday

- Berry and Pistachio Yogurt ❋ Citrus-Spiked Fat Burner Drink
- Chicken Kebabs with Cucumber Radish Salad
- Oven Ratatouille with Millet

Thursday

- Radish and Cheese Spread on Pumpernickel ❋ Raspberry and Mango Salad
- Marinated Asparagus with Turkey
- Sole with Spring Vegetables

Friday

- Bread with Three-Berry Jam ❋ Tomato and Red Pepper Mix
- Seafood Cocktail with Broccoli
- Boiled Potatoes with Veggie-Garlic Dip

Saturday

- Avocado with Tomato Cottage Cheese ❋ Blackberry Sorbet
- Kohlrabi and Mushroom Carpaccio
- Tuna Kebabs with Saffron Rice

Sunday

- Tropical Fruits with Coconut Lime Yogurt ❋ Rocket Dip with Crispbread
- Tomato and Apple Salad with Rocket
- Bean Sprouts and Chicken Stir-Fry

Berry and

Start your day with

Pistachio

fruit and protein

Yogurt

Serves 2: • 250 g (9 oz) mixed berries or grapes • 2 tsp lemon juice • 1 tbsp apple juice concentrate • 4 tsp pistachio nuts • 300 g (10 oz) low-fat natural yogurt

Rinse the fruit briefly, drain, and sort. Cut large fruit into smaller pieces. Toss the berries with the lemon juice and apple juice concentrate. Chop the pistachios and stir them into the yogurt. Arrange alternating layers of berries and yogurt in small glass dishes, saving one-third of the berries to sprinkle on top.

power

POWER PER SERVING: 151 CALORIES • 7 G PROTEIN • 5 G FAT • 21 G CARBOHYDRATE

Tropical Fruits with Coconut Lime Yogurt

The selenium in coconut makes you cheerful

Serves 2: • 1 papaya • 1 star fruit • 1 kiwi • 200 g (7 oz) low-fat vanilla yogurt • 2 tbsp unsweetened coconut milk • 2 tsp brown sugar • 1 tbsp lime juice • 2 tsp grated coconut, toasted

Peel the papaya, remove the seeds and slice. Wash and slice the star fruit. Peel the kiwi and cut it into wedges. Arrange the fruit decoratively on a plate. Mix the yogurt with the coconut milk, sugar, and lime juice. Drizzle the coconut mixture over the fruit or serve it in a bowl alongside. Garnish with the grated coconut.

power

Power per serving: 170 calories • 14 g protein • 2 g fat • 23 g carbohydrate

Apple and Raspberry Muesli with Yogurt

A real brain food combination

Serves 2: • 2 tbsp pumpkin seeds • 4 tbsp rolled oats • 1 tbsp raisins • 1 apple • 1 tbsp lemon juice • 100 g (4 oz) fresh raspberries • 375 ml (12 fl oz) probiotic yogurt (healthfood shop) • 2 tsp maple syrup

Toast the pumpkin seeds and mix them with the oats and raisins. Divide the mixture between two small bowls. Peel the apple and grate it, avoiding the core. Toss the grated apple with the lemon juice. Briefly rinse the raspberries, removing any foreign matter. Mix the yogurt and maple syrup. Sprinkle the apples and raspberries on the oat mixture, and pour the yogurt over.

power

Power per serving: 280 calories • 12 g protein • 10 g fat • 34 g carbohydrate

Bread with Three-Berry Jam

Fat burner jam to feed your sweet tooth

Rinse the berries briefly, sort and trim them, and cut into small pieces. In a saucepan, simmer the berries, fructose, and ascorbic acid for 5 minutes over low heat.

Stir the agar-agar into the cold water, add it to the saucepan, and simmer for 2–3 minutes. Immediately transfer the berry jam to two small glass jars with screw tops. Seal them tightly and leave to cool.

Tip: Sterilize the jars first by boiling the jars and the lids in water for 5 minutes; fill them while still hot.

Spread 1 tablespoon of the cream cheese and 2 tablespoons of the jam on each slice of bread. Garnish with lemon balm. Store the remaining jam in the refrigerator and consume as quickly as possible.

Serves 2:

250 g (9 oz) mixed ripe berries
60 g (2 1/2 oz) fructose (healthfood shop)
1 tsp granulated ascorbic acid (healthfood shop)
1/2 tsp agar-agar (vegetable gelling agent – healthfood shop)
2 tbsp cold water
2 tbsp low-fat cream cheese
2 slices wholemeal bread
1 sprig fresh lemon balm

Wholemeal Bread

White bread has a high glycaemic index and is a true fat storer. On the other hand, most whole-grain breads are fat burners. Whenever possible, spread your wholemeal bread with low-fat cream cheese as an accompaniment to jam instead of butter. Wholemeal bread also goes well with vegetables and salad.

Power per serving:

240 calories

5 g protein • 2 g fat

52 g carbohydrate

power

Wholemeal Rolls with Tomato

The secret to eternal youth, from Crete

Thoroughly mash the herb paté with a fork and mix it with the tomato purée, lemon juice, and olive oil until smooth. Season to taste with pepper and salt.

Serves 2:
50 g (2 oz) vegetarian herb paté (healthfood shop)
3 tsp tomato purée
1 tsp lemon juice
1 tsp olive oil
Black pepper to taste
Salt to taste
2 wholemeal rolls
2 tomatoes
2 sprigs fresh basil

Slice the rolls in half horizontally, and spread the paté mixture on all of the halves, dividing evenly.

Wash the tomatoes, remove the cores, and cut them into small wedges.

Arrange the tomato wedges on the roll halves. Sprinkle with a little salt and pepper. Wash the basil, shake it dry, pull off the leaves and use them to garnish the rolls.

Tomatoes

Tomatoes raise your spirits, are a tonic for your heart and liver, and help prevent gout and rheumatism. They contain the antioxidant lycopene, which helps prevent cancer. Tomatoes also contain minerals that stimulate fat burning, including magnesium, calcium, iron, and zinc. They also contain potassium, which is a natural diuretic.

power

POWER PER SERVING:
196 CALORIES
8 G PROTEIN • 5 G FAT
30 G CARBOHYDRATE

Radish Cheese Spread on Pumpernickel

Spicy slices of vital nutrients

Serves 2: • 1 tsp butter, softened • 1/2 tsp French mustard • 2 large slices pumpernickel bread • 50 g (2 oz) radishes • 50 g (2 oz) Camembert cheese • Black pepper to taste

Mix the butter and mustard and spread it on the pumpernickel slices. Wash and trim the radishes. Cut the radishes and Camembert into thin slices. Arrange the radishes and Camembert in an overlapping pattern on the slices of bread. Season with freshly ground black pepper.

power

Power per serving: 152 calories • 10 g protein • 6 g fat • 15 g carbohydrate

Smoked Salmon with Horseradish and Apple

Fish – a superior fat burner

Serves 2: • 2 tbsp low-fat cream cheese • 1 tsp grated fresh horseradish • 1/4 medium apple • 2 tsp lemon juice • 2 slices rye bread • 2 sprigs fresh dill • 50 g (2 oz) smoked salmon • Black pepper

Mix the cream cheese with the horseradish and a little pepper. Wash the apple, slice thinly, and immediately drizzle it with the lemon juice. Spread the horseradish mixture on the slices of bread and cut them in half diagonally. Wash the dill and shake it dry. Arrange the apple slices, smoked salmon, and dill sprigs on the bread, dividing evenly.

power

Power per serving: 158 calories • 10 g protein • 6 g fat • 15 g carbohydrate

Avocado with Tomato Cottage Cheese

A recipe for beauty, a slender figure, and healthy nerves

Wash and quarter the tomato, remove the seeds and core, and cut it into small cubes. Cut the avocado in half and remove the stone. Scoop out the avocado flesh from the peel with a large spoon, leaving only a thin layer inside the peel. Dice the flesh and immediately drizzle the lemon juice over the avocado halves and diced avocado.

Mix the cottage cheese with the diced tomato and diced avocado. Season with a little salt and pepper. Transfer the mixture to the hollowed-out avocado halves, sprinkle with the chopped chives, and serve.

Serves 2:

1 tomato
1 ripe avocado
2 tsp fresh lemon juice
100 g (4 oz) cottage cheese
Salt to taste
Black pepper to taste
1 tbsp chopped fresh chives

Avocados

Although this green exotic is the fattiest of fruits, it is loaded with unsaturated fatty acids that are essential to a healthy diet. They promote soft skin, healthy cell walls, and strong nerves, and program your body's hormones to burn fat. Eat avocados and the fat-storing hormone, insulin, doesn't stand a chance.

POWER PER SERVING:

394 CALORIES

10 G PROTEIN • 38 G FAT

2 G CARBOHYDRATE

power

Raw Vegetables with Herby Cream Cheese

Dip into vitality

Mix together the cream cheese, mineral water, lemon juice, salt and pepper, and stir until smooth. Peel and crush the garlic. Wash the parsley, shake it dry, and set several leaves aside. Finely chop the remaining parsley leaves. Stir the chopped parsley and garlic into the cream cheese mixture.

Trim and wash the radishes. Trim and wash the celery and cut it into slices. Cut the yellow pepper in half and remove the stem, ribs, and seeds, then wash it and cut it into strips. Cut the bread into small triangles.

Arrange the radishes, celery, and pepper strips around the dip. Garnish with the remaining parsley leaves and serve with the bread triangles.

Serves 2:

100 g (4 oz) low-fat cream cheese
2 tbsp mineral water
2 tsp lemon juice
Salt to taste
Black pepper to taste
1 clove garlic
Fresh Italian parsley
100 g (4 oz) radishes
2 celery stalks
1 small yellow pepper
1 slice rye bread

power

POWER PER SERVING: 122 CALORIES • 11 G PROTEIN • 1 G FAT • 16 G CARBOHYDRATE

Rocket Dip with Crispbread

Triggers a flood of "happiness hormones"

Serves 2: • 75 g (3 oz) rocket • 2 tbsp pumpkin seeds • 2 tbsp freshly grated Parmesan cheese • 2 tsp balsamic vinegar • 2 tbsp olive oil • 4–5 tbsp vegetable stock • Salt • Black pepper • 1 spring onion • 2 slices rye crispbread

Trim, sort, wash, and chop the rocket. Place the rocket, pumpkin seeds, Parmesan, vinegar, and olive oil in a blender or food processor, and process to a smooth purée. Stir in the stock to form a creamy paste, and season with salt and pepper. Wash and trim the spring onion, slice it into fine rings, and add it to the paste. Break up the crispbread and use it for dipping.

power

POWER PER SERVING: 262 CALORIES • 9 G PROTEIN • 22 G FAT • 11 G CARBOHYDRATE

Red Pepper and Pineapple Salsa

Fat-burning enzymes do their part

Serves 2: • 300 g (10 oz) pineapple • 1/2 red pepper • 1/2 small red onion • 1 tbsp lime juice • Salt • Tabasco sauce • 2 tsp olive oil • 1 tbsp chopped fresh coriander • 2 slices wholemeal toast

Peel the pineapple and cut it into small cubes, avoiding the tough core. Wash and trim the red pepper, and dice it finely. Peel the onion and chop it finely. Stir together the pineapple, pepper, onion, lime juice, salt, Tabasco, olive oil, and coriander. Serve with the wholemeal toast.

power

POWER PER SERVING: 95 CALORIES • 1 G PROTEIN • 5 G FAT • 12 G CARBOHYDRATE

Tomato Stuffed wi
Radish Yogurt

Essential oils keep you fit

Serves 2: • 2 large, ripe tomatoes • 100 g (4 oz) radishes • 150 g (6oz) low-fat natural yogurt • • 2 tbsp chopped fresh chives • Salt to taste • Black pepper to taste • 1 tsp lemon juice

Wash the tomatoes. Slice off the top of each tomato and scoop out the tomato flesh with a spoon. Wash and grate the radishes. Mix the grated radishes with the yogurt and 1 tablespoon of the chives. Season the mixture with salt, pepper, and lemon juice. Fill the tomatoes with the radish and yogurt mixture and sprinkle with the remaining chives.

POWER PER SERVING: 64 CALORIES • 5 G PROTEIN • 1 G FAT • 9 G CARBOHYDRATE

Courgette slices with Mushrooms

A deposit in your health account

Serves 2: • 75 g (3 oz) button mushrooms • 1 spring onion • 2 tsp fresh lemon juice • 1 tsp balsamic vinegar • 1 1/2 tbsp olive oil • Salt to taste • Black pepper to taste • 200 g (8 oz) courgettes

Trim, wash, and slice the mushrooms and spring onion. Mix them with the lemon juice, vinegar, 1 tablespoon of the olive oil, salt, and pepper. Trim and wash the courgettes, cut into thick slices, and season with salt. Brush a frying pan with the remaining oil and sauté the courgette slices for a few minutes on both sides. Season with salt and pepper. Arrange the courgette slices on serving plates and top with the mushrooms.

POWER PER SERVING: 87 CALORIES • 3 G PROTEIN • 7 G FAT • 3 G CARBOHYDRATE

Ham-Wrapped Asparagus with Basil Dip

These slender stalks are true fat burners

Serves 2:
300 g (10 oz) asparagus
Salt to taste
1 tsp olive oil
100 g (4 oz) low-fat natural yogurt
2 tbsp sour cream
1 tsp capers (drained)
1 tsp fresh lemon juice
Black pepper to taste
12 fresh basil leaves
50 g (2 oz) lean smoked ham

Wash the asparagus, break off the woody ends, and peel the bottom third of the stalks. In a saucepan, bring a generous amount of salted water to a boil with the oil. Add the asparagus, cover, reduce the heat, and simmer until tender, about 10–12 minutes.

For the dip, mix the yogurt and sour cream. Finely chop the capers and mix them in. Season the dip with lemon juice, salt, and pepper. Wash and shake dry the basil leaves and set several leaves aside. Chop the remaining leaves finely and mix them into the dip. Drain the asparagus, plunge it into ice water to stop the cooking, and drain again.

Wrap a slice of ham around each asparagus stalk and arrange on a platter. Garnish the dip with the remaining basil.

Lighten Up Your Sauces

125 ml (4 fl oz) of cream contains 31 g of fat, and the same amount of crème fraîche contains 40 g of fat. Instead of using these, lighten up your sauces. Try puréed vegetables, which have a delicate taste and a smooth texture. Or replace the cream with low-fat buttermilk, sour cream, or yogurt.

Power per serving:
185 calories
9 g protein • 14 g fat
6 g carbohydrate

power

Cucumber and Prawn Salad

The best fat burners come from the sea

Thaw the peas. Toast the sunflower kernels until golden brown in an ungreased frying pan. Peel, dice, and lightly salt the cucumber. Rinse the prawns and drain. Wash the lettuce, shake it dry, and tear it into bite-sized pieces. Wash the dill, shake it dry, and set aside 2–3 sprigs. Remove the leaves from the remaining sprigs and chop.

In a large bowl, stir together the yogurt, lemon juice, and corn oil until smooth. Season with salt and pepper. Add the peas, cucumber, prawns, lettuce, and dill to the bowl and toss well.

Divide the salad between two serving plates, sprinkle with sunflower seeds, garnish with the remaining dill, and serve with pumpernickel crackers.

Serves 2:

- 60 g (2 oz) frozen peas
- 2 tsp sunflower kernels
- Salt to taste
- 200 g (7 oz) cucumber
- 80 g (3 oz) prawns, peeled and cooked
- 2 lollo rosso leaves
- A few sprigs of fresh dill
- 125 ml (4 fl oz) probiotic yogurt (healthfood shop)
- 1 tsp fresh lemon juice
- 1 tsp corn oil
- Black pepper to taste
- Pumpernickel crackers

Prawns for Taurine

Prawns provide taurine, a protein substance that helps the pituitary gland to send out its fat-melting hormones, such as the growth hormone that builds up muscles and breaks down fat. This valuable fat burner can also be found in mussels, poultry, and liver.

Power per serving:
166 calories
14 g protein • 6 g fat
14 g carbohydrate

power

Raspberry and Mango Salad

Snack yourself to slenderness

Serves 2: • 1 ripe mango • 150 g (6 oz) fresh raspberries • 50 g (2 oz) low-fat cottage cheese • 100 g (4 oz) low-fat natural yogurt • 1 tsp honey • 2 tsp pine nuts, toasted • 1 sprig fresh mint

Peel the mango, cut it into thin wedges, and arrange them on a serving dish. Rinse the raspberries briefly, sort them, and sprinkle them over the mango wedges. Stir together the cottage cheese, yogurt, and honey and pour over the top. Sprinkle with pine nuts. Wash the mint, remove the leaves from the stem, and use them to garnish the salad.

power

POWER PER SERVING: 199 CALORIES • 6 G PROTEIN • 7 G FAT • 23 G CARBOHYDRATE

Blackberry Sorbert

A craving for ice cream? Go right ahead!

Serves 2: • 250 g (9 oz) fresh blackberries • 2 tsp lemon juice • 1 tbsp maple syrup • 50 ml (2 fl oz) water • 1 sprig fresh lemon balm

Wash and drain the blackberries. Set a few berries aside and purée the rest together with the lemon juice, maple syrup, and water. Place the blackberry purée in a stainless steel bowl, cover, and freeze for 3–4 hours, stirring at 1-hour intervals. Transfer the sorbet to dessert bowls, and garnish with the remaining berries and lemon balm.

power

POWER PER SERVING: 82 CALORIES • 2 G PROTEIN • 1 G FAT • 14 G CARBOHYDRATE

Strawberries with Two Dips

Fruit for your sweet tooth

Rinse, drain, and sort the strawberries.

For the chocolate dip, chop the chocolate coarsely. Place it in a heat-proof bowl with 3 tablespoons of the milk. Put the bowl over a saucepan of water and heat until the chocolate has melted, stirring constantly. Leave the chocolate dip to cool.

For the vanilla dip, slit open the vanilla pod lengthways, scrape out the seeds with a small knife, and mix them with the honey, the remaining 1 tablespoon of milk, and the yogurt.

Arrange the strawberries decoratively on a plate, and serve them with the chocolate and vanilla dips.

Serves 2:

250 g (9 oz) fresh strawberries
30 g (1 oz) unsweetened chocolate
4 tbsp low-fat milk
1/2 vanilla pod
1 tsp floral honey
60 g (2 oz) low-fat vanilla yogurt

power

POWER PER SERVING:
158 CALORIES
7 G PROTEIN • 5 G FAT
20 G CARBOHYDRATE

Kiwi and Strawberry Shake with Mint

A sweet fat burner cocktail

Makes 2 drinks: • 1 kiwi • 100 g (4 oz) fresh strawberries • 2 tsp chopped fresh mint • Juice from 1 lime • 2 tsp maple syrup • 2 tbsp instant porridge flakes • 250 ml (8 fl oz) cold milk

Peel and dice the kiwi. Wash and trim the strawberries and cut them into small pieces. Put the mint, lime juice, maple syrup, and porridge flakes, and half the milk in a blender and blend for about 15 seconds. Add the rest of the milk and blend vigorously again. Pour into two large glasses and serve with fat straws.

power

POWER PER DRINK: 83 CALORIES • 2 G PROTEIN • 1 G FAT • 17 G CARBOHYDRATE

Tomato and Red Pepper Mix

A spicy fat burner cocktail

Makes 2 drinks: • 75 g (3 oz) red pepper • 75 g (3 oz) celeriac • 2 tbsp chopped fresh Italian parsley • 1/2 tsp chilli powder • 300 ml (10 fl oz) cold tomato juice • Salt • Black pepper • 4 ice cubes

Trim and wash the red pepper, peel the celeriac, and dice both vegetables. Put the red pepper, celeriac, parsley, chilli powder, and 125 ml (4 fl oz) of the tomato juice in a blender and purée. Add the remaining juice and blend vigorously. Season with salt and pepper. Put the ice cubes in two glasses, pour the mixture over the top, and serve with fat straws.

power

POWER PER DRINK: 50 CALORIES • 3 G PROTEIN • 1 G FAT • 8 G CARBOHYDRATE

Citrus-Spiked Fat Burner Drink

The slimming power of tropical fruits

Plunge the tomatoes into boiling water for a few seconds, then into iced water, drain, and pull off their skins. Cut the tomatoes in half and squeeze out the seeds. Chop the tomatoes coarsely. Trim the carrot, peel, and grate it finely. Remove the seeds from the papaya half, peel, and dice it. Put the tomatoes, carrot, and papaya in a blender. Squeeze the juice from the oranges and lemon, and add to the blender. Add the fructose, ascorbic acid, and olive oil. Blend for 15 seconds at high speed.

Pour the drink into two tall glasses. Cut part-way into the lemon slices and place one on the rim of each glass. Serve with fat straws.

Makes 2 drinks:

2 ripe tomatoes
1 medium carrot
1/2 ripe papaya
2 oranges
1 lemon
1 tsp fructose (healthfood shop)
Dash of ascorbic acid granules (healthfood shop)
1 tsp olive oil
2 slices lemon

Tropical Fruits for Enzymes

Papaya, pineapple, and mango provide enzymes that indirectly boost fat burning. These enzymes break down protein and help transport valuable fat burners to your cells where they do their job of promoting health and fitness.

POWER PER DRINK:
153 CALORIES
4 G PROTEIN • 3 G FAT
32 G CARBOHYDRATE

power

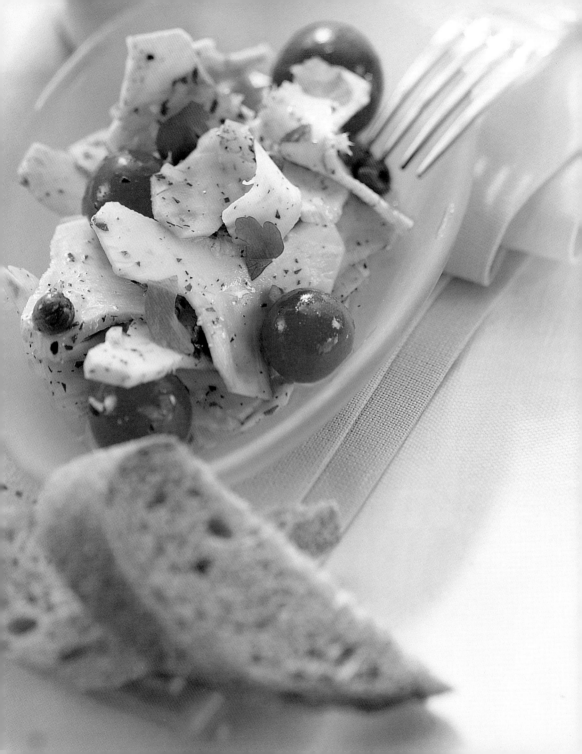

Artichoke and Cherry Tomato Salad

Essential fatty acids trigger fat-burning hormones

Add the lemon juice to a medium bowl of water. Break the stems off the artichokes. Cut off the top third of the artichoke leaves. Pull out the inner leaves and the inedible hairy centre to expose the heart. Trim the hearts and immediately place them in the lemon water.

For the salad dressing, whisk together the vinegar, herb salt, and pepper. Gradually whisk in the olive oil, corn oil, and sunflower oil.

Drain the artichoke hearts, cut them into very thin strips, and mix them with the dressing.

Meanwhile, peel the shallot and garlic and chop both finely. Wash the cherry tomatoes. Cut the larger ones in half and remove the stems. Add the shallot, garlic, tomatoes, capers, and parsley to the bowl with the artichokes and mix well. Season the salad generously with salt and pepper.

Serves 2:

Juice of 1/2 lemon
2 small artichokes (about 500 g (18 oz))
1 1/2 tbsp white wine vinegar
Herb salt to taste
Black pepper to taste
2 tbsp olive oil
1 tsp corn oil
1 tsp sunflower oil
1 shallot
1 clove garlic
225 g (8 oz) cherry tomatoes
1 tsp capers (drained)
2 tbsp chopped fresh Italian parsley

power

POWER PER SERVING: 217 CALORIES • 3 G PROTEIN • 18 G FAT • 13 G CARBOHYDRATE

Kohlrabi and Mushroom Carpaccio

Raw food for nutrition and energy

Serves 2: • 1 tbsp sesame seeds • 300 g (10 oz) kohlrabi • 50 g (2 oz) mushrooms • 1 tbsp white wine vinegar • 1 spring onion • Salt • Black pepper • 2 tbsp sunflower oil • 1/2 tsp sesame oil • Wholemeal bread

Toast the sesame seeds in a dry non-stick frying pan. Peel the kohlrabi, cut it into quarters, slice it thinly, and arrange on two plates. Clean the mushrooms and cut them into very thin slices. Wash and trim the spring onion and cut it into rings. Scatter the mushrooms and spring onion over the kohlrabi. Whisk together the vinegar, salt, pepper, sunflower oil, and sesame oil, and drizzle it over the top. Sprinkle with the toasted sesame seeds. Serve with wholemeal bread.

power

Power per serving: 150 calories • 5 g protein • 12 g fat • 7 g carbohydrate

Tomato and Apple Salad with Rocket

With fat-burning fruits and vegetables

Serves 2: • 4 ripe tomatoes • 1/2 tart apple • 1 carrot • 30 g (1 oz) rocket • 1 tbsp lemon juice • 1 tsp balsamic vinegar • Salt to taste • Black pepper to taste • 2 tbsp olive oil • 30 g (1 oz) Parmesan cheese • Wholemeal bread

Wash the tomatoes and cut each into 8 wedges. Cut the apple in half, remove the core, and cut into slices. Peel and grate the carrot. Rinse the rocket, shake dry, remove the stems, and chop. Whisk together the lemon juice, vinegar, salt, pepper, and olive oil. Toss the tomatoes, apple, grated carrot, and rocket in the dressing. Use a vegetable peeler to shave the Parmesan over the top. Serve with wholemeal bread.

power

Power per serving: 221 calories • 8 g protein • 18 g fat • 8 g carbohydrate

Tex-Mex Salad with Kidney Beans

With the fat-burning factor methionine

Rinse and drain the beans. Cut the yellow pepper in half, remove the stem, ribs, and seeds, and wash and cut it into strips. Cut the avocado in half, then remove the stone and peel. Cut the avocado halves into narrow wedges and drizzle them with the lemon juice.

Wash and trim the celery and cut it into thin diagonal slices. Peel the onion, cut it in half, then cut it into thin slices.

Whisk together the vinegar, salt, black pepper, Tabasco, and oil in a medium bowl. Wash the parsley or coriander, shake it dry, chop it, and add to the dressing. Stir in the vegetables and beans. Wash the lettuce, shake it dry, and arrange on serving plates. Spoon the vegetables on top of the lettuce leaves.

Serves 2:

100 g (4 oz) tinned red kidney beans (drained)
1 yellow pepper
1 avocado
1 tsp lemon juice
1 celery stalk
1 small red onion
2 tbsp red wine vinegar
Salt to taste
Black pepper to taste
Tabasco sauce to taste
3 tbsp olive oil
a few springs of fresh coriander or Italian parsley
4 iceberg lettuce leaves

Legumes for Methionine

Methionine is an important substance for building up protein. A deficiency weakens your immune system, increases your risk of cancer, and causes you to put on weight. Without methionine, there would be no formation of carnitine, which transports fat from your hips to be combusted in your muscles. Good sources of methionine include legumes, fish, poultry, and cheese.

Power per serving:

377 calories

5 g protein • 35 g fat

12 g carbohydrate

Curried Veal Fillet with Tomato Yogurt

A hearty way to lose weight

Wash the tomato, cut it in half, squeeze out the seeds, and dice the flesh finely. Peel the onion and dice it finely. Mix together the tomatoes, onion, and yogurt. Wash the parsley, shake it dry, chop it finely, and mix half of it into the tomato yogurt. Season with salt, pepper, coriander, and lemon juice; cover and refrigerate.

Serves 2:

1 medium tomato
1 small red onion
200 g (7 oz) low-fat natural yogurt
5 sprigs fresh Italian parsley
Salt to taste
Black pepper to taste
1/2 tsp ground coriander
2 tsp lemon juice
500 ml (8 fl oz) vegetable stock
200 g (7 oz) boneless veal
1 tsp curry powder
Dark rye bread

Bring the vegetable stock to the boil in a deep frying pan. Cut the veal into thin slices, rub each slice with a little curry powder, and place in the pan. Reduce the heat to low and simmer the veal for about 5 minutes. Remove the meat, and season with salt and pepper. Sprinkle with the remaining parsley. Serve the veal with the tomato yogurt and dark rye bread.

Sour Helpers

Vinegar and lemon juice are true slenderizers. Eating a salad with vinegar before a meal of fish, or sprinkling lemon juice over a chicken breast or turkey escalope, helps your stomach break down protein and helps your body metabolize it better, thus speeding it to its final destination – the 70 billion cells in your body – where it can do its slenderizing work.

Power per serving

213 calories

27 g protein • 5 g fat

13 g carbohydrate

power

Marinated Asparagus with Turkey

Asparagus reduces weight and blood pressure

Wash the asparagus, break off the woody ends, and peel the lower third of the stalks. Bring a pan of salted water to the boil. Add the asparagus, reduce the heat, and simmer until tender, for about 10–12 minutes.

Serves 2:

- **500 g (18 oz) asparagus**
- **Salt to taste**
- **1 hard-boiled egg**
- **2 tsp pine nuts**
- **2 tbsp lemon juice**
- **1 tbsp white wine vinegar**
- **Black pepper to taste**
- **2 tbsp olive oil**
- **100 g (4 oz) cherry tomatoes**
- **8 fresh basil leaves**
- **50 g (2 oz) sliced smoked turkey breast**

Toast the pine nuts in a dry non-stick frying pan, until golden brown. Drain the asparagus, setting aside 3 tablespoons of the asparagus water.

For the marinade, whisk together the lemon juice, vinegar, salt, black pepper, oil, and reserved asparagus water. Pour the marinade over the asparagus in a shallow dish and refrigerate for 2–3 hours.

Peel the hard-boiled egg and cut it into 8 wedges. Wash the tomatoes and cut them in half. Wash and shake dry the basil, and chop the leaves coarsely. Arrange the egg wedges, tomatoes, and turkey breast alongside the asparagus on serving plates. Sprinkle with the pine nuts and basil.

Skinny Sticks

From April to June you can let yourself go and fill up with asparagus. These skinny sticks contain only 15 calories per 100 g (4 oz). The asparagine in asparagus stimulates your kidneys, acting as a natural diuretic. Other fat-burning factors in asparagus are fibre, vitamin C, iron, calcium, and iodine.

Power per serving

260 calories

15 g protein • 19 g fat

9 g carbohydrate

power

Chicken Kebabs w
Poultry + lemon = a perfect fat-burning combination
Cucumber Radish S

Serves 2: • 200 g (7 oz) boneless, skinless chicken breast • 250 g (9 oz) cucumber • 2 tbsp lemon juice • Salt • Black pepper • 2 tbsp olive oil • 250 g (9 oz) radishes • 2 tbsp chopped Italian parsley • 1 tsp chilli powder

Cut the chicken breast into cubes and thread them on to 2 wooden skewers. In a shallow dish, mix together 1 tablespoon of the lemon juice, salt, pepper, and 1/2 tablespoon of the oil. Coat the chicken kebabs well with the marinade. Peel the cucumber, wash and trim the radishes, and slice them. Mix the remaining lemon juice and oil, salt, pepper, and chilli powder. Add the cucumber, radishes, and parsley, and toss well. Bake the kebabs in the oven for 8–10 minutes and serve with the salad.

POWER PER SERVING: 283 CALORIES • 26 G PROTEIN • 16 G FAT • 6 G CARBOHYDRATE

Courgette Strips
Loaded with omega-3 fatty acids
with Smoked Salmon

Serves 2: • 300 g (10 oz) courgettes• 2 tbsp olive oil • Salt • Black pepper • 2 tsp balsamic vinegar • 100 g (4 oz) sliced smoked salmon • 2 tbsp low-fat natural yogurt • 2 slices wholemeal bread

Wash and trim the courgettes, then cut them lengthways into thin slices. Brush a non-stick frying pan with some of the oil, add the courgette slices a few at a time, and sauté for 2–3 minutes on each side over medium heat. Transfer the courgettes to a shallow bowl, sprinkle with salt, black pepper, vinegar, and the remaining oil, and marinate for 2 hours. Serve with the smoked salmon, yogurt, and bread.

POWER PER SERVING: 300 CALORIES • 17 G PROTEIN • 24 G FAT • 4 G CARBOHYDRATE

Seafood Cocktail with Broccoli

An extra-light feast

Cut the cod into strips and the squid into pieces. Rinse the mussels, pull off any hairy filaments, and discard any that are open. In a saucepan, bring 125 ml (4 fl oz) water to the boil. Simmer the fish strips and squid in the water for 2–3 minutes over low heat; remove them from the water and set aside. Place the mussels in the cooking liquid, cover the pot, and simmer for about 3–5 minutes, until the shells open. Remove the mussels from the stock and pull the mussel meat from the shells. Discard any unopened mussels.

Trim the broccoli and blanch it for 3 minutes in boiling, salted water. Plunge the broccoli into cold water and drain. Wash the red pepper, removed the ribs and seeds, and cut it into strips. Trim the spring onion, wash it, and slice it.

In a medium bowl, whisk together the soy sauce, lemon juice, sugar, salt, and pepper. Stir the coriander or parsley, cod strips, squid, mussels, and vegetables into the marinade. Serve with the baguette.

Serves 2:

100 g (4 oz) cod fillet
100 g (4 oz) squid rings or tentacles (cleaned)
300 g (10 oz) fresh mussels (in the shell)
300 g (10 oz) broccoli
Salt to taste
1 small red pepper
1 spring onion
2 tbsp soy sauce
2 tbsp lemon juice
1 tsp brown sugar
Black pepper to taste
1 tbsp chopped fresh coriander or Italian parsley
Wholemeal baguette

Seafood: The Super Fat Burner

The protein in seafood stimulates fat burning. Seafood provides you with an abundance of tyrosine, an amino acid that your body uses to produce the fat-burning hormones norepinephrine and dopamine. Seafood also provides iodine, the fuel for an active thyroid.

POWER PER SERVING:

159 CALORIES

25 G PROTEIN • 2 G FAT

10 G CARBOHYDRATE

power

Spaghetti with Herb Pesto

Laced with three herbs

Plunge the tomatoes into boiling water for a few seconds, transfer them to iced water, drain, and pull off their skins. Cut the tomatoes into quarters, remove the seeds, and cut the flesh into small cubes. In a saucepan, bring a generous amount of salted water to the boil, and cook the spaghetti until it is al dente.

For the pesto, rinse the chervil, parsley, and basil, shake dry, remove the leaves from the stems, and chop them coarsely. Peel and crush the garlic. Put the chervil, parsley, basil, garlic, vinegar, almonds, and Parmesan in a blender or food processor. Add 4–6 tablespoons of water from the spaghetti and process into a fine purée. Gradually drizzle in the oil, and season to taste with salt and pepper.

Drain the pasta and add the diced tomato, salt, and pepper. Add the pesto to taste, toss well, and serve.

Serves 2:

500 g (18 oz) tomatoes
Salt to taste
150 g (5 oz) whole-wheat spaghetti
Handful of fresh chervil
Handful of fresh Italian parsley
6 large fresh basil leaves
1 small clove garlic
2 tsp balsamic vinegar
2 tbsp chopped almonds
25 g (1 oz) Parmesan cheese, grated
2 tbsp olive oil
Black pepper to taste

Herbs

Herbs magically transform dishes, maintain your health, calm and relax you, stimulate you, and keep you thin. Mixing herbs in recipes gives you maximum nutritional benefit. For example, in the pesto above, chervil promotes circulation and aids digestion; parsley activates your metabolism; and basil fortifies and soothes your stomach.

POWER PER SERVING:

434 CALORIES

17 G PROTEIN • 4 G FAT

41 G CARBOHYDRATE

power

Boiled Potatoes with Veggie-Garlic Dip

High-glycaemic and low-fat

Scrub the potatoes and boil them in salted water until tender (about 20–25 minutes). Remove the stem, ribs, and seeds from the pepper, wash it and cut into cubes. Peel the cucumber and dice it finely. Trim the spring onions, wash, and cut into fine rings. Peel and crush the garlic. Mix together the cream cheese, milk, and lemon juice, and season generously with salt and paprika. Add the diced pepper and cucumber, garlic, and two-thirds of the spring onion. Wash and shake dry the dill, chop all but a few sprigs, and stir it into the cream cheese mixture. Garnish the cream cheese mixture with the remaining spring onions and dill.

Drain the potatoes, wait until they're cool enough to handle, peel them, and serve with the dip.

Serves 2:

- 400 g (14 oz) small potatoes
- Salt to taste
- 1/2 red pepper
- 100 g (4 oz) cucumber
- 2 spring onions
- 1 small clove garlic
- 250 g (9 oz) low-fat cream cheese
- 3 tbsp low-fat milk
- 2 tsp lemon juice
- 1/2 tsp paprika
- Handful of fresh dill

Potatoes

Potatoes have a high glycaemic index. Combine them with fat and the insulin weight gain is complete. That's why we suggest you use a lighter version: 100 g (4 oz) of boiled potatoes have 0.3 g of fat, Chips fatten your figure with up to 40 g of fat. To combat their fat-storing potential, eat potatoes with low-fat cream cheese, lean fish, poultry, or vegetables.

Power per serving:

243 calories

23 g protein • 1 g fat

35 g carbohydrate

Oven Ratatouille with Millet

Pamper your body with lots of vegetables

Preheat the oven to 225°C (450°F, Gas Mark 8). Cut the peppers into quarters. Remove the stems, ribs, and seeds, and wash and cut them into pieces. Wash and trim the courgettes and aubergine. Cut the courgettes into slices and the aubergine into large cubes. Peel the onion and chop it coarsely. Wash the tomatoes, cut them into quarters, remove the seeds, and cut them into pieces. Peel and chop the garlic.

Grease a casserole with 1 tablespoon of the oil and heat in the oven for 5 minutes. Put the vegetables in the casserole and season with salt, pepper, and the herbes de Provence. Drizzle the vegetables with the remaining 1 tablespoon oil and the lemon juice. In the meantime, bring 125 ml (4 fl oz) of the stock to the boil and pour it over the vegetables. Bake the vegetables in the middle of the oven for 30 minutes, stirring occasionally.

Bring the remaining stock to the boil, add the millet, and cook for 25 minutes over low heat, until the millet is tender. Stir in the parsley and season with salt and pepper. Serve the cooked millet with the ratatouille.

Serves 2:

1 small red pepper
1 small green pepper
100 g (4 oz) courgettes
100 g (4 oz) aubergine
1/2 medium onion
200 g (8 oz) plum tomatoes
2 cloves garlic
2 tbsp olive oil
Salt to taste
Black pepper to taste
1 tsp herbes de Provence
1 tbsp lemon juice
375 ml (12 fl oz) vegetable stock
125 g (5 oz) millet
2 tbsp chopped fresh Italian parsley

power

POWER PER SERVING: 464 CALORIES • 11 G PROTEIN • 19 G FAT • 61 G CARBOHYDRATE

Gazpacho with Croutons

Carotenoids in tomatoes and peppers keep you fit

Serves 2:

2 slices stale wholemeal bread
Salt to taste
200 g (7 oz) tomato
1 small red pepper
1 small green pepper
100 g (4 oz) cucumber
1 clove garlic
1 tsp tomato purée
250 ml (8 fl oz) cold tomato juice
3 tbsp vegetable stock
2 tsp olive oil
1–2 tsp lemon juice
1 tsp brown sugar
Cayenne pepper to taste

Cut 1 slice of bread into cubes, sprinkle with salt, and soak in a teaspoon of lukewarm water. In the meantime, plunge the tomatoes into boiling water for a few seconds, then into iced water, and pull off the skins. Cut the tomatoes in half, squeeze out the seeds, and chop the flesh coarsely. Remove the stems, ribs, and seeds from the peppers, and wash and dice them. Peel the cucumber, cut it in half lengthways, scrape out the seeds with a spoon, and dice. Peel and chop the garlic.

Put the soaked bread, tomatoes, garlic, the tomato purée, tomato juice, stock, and half each of the red pepper, green pepper, and cucumber, in a blender or food processor. Add 1 teaspoon of the olive oil, the lemon juice, sugar, salt, and cayenne pepper. Blend until the mixture is smooth. Cover and refrigerate for 1 hour.

Cut the remaining slice of bread into small cubes. Heat the remaining 1 tablespoon of olive oil in a frying pan. Add the bread cubes and sauté until golden brown. Stir the puréed mixture, pour it into two soup bowls, and sprinkle with the remaining diced vegetables and the croutons.

power

Power per serving: 166 calories • 5 g protein • 6 g fat • 22 g carbohydrate

Risotto with Raw Vegetables

Stay slim with whole-grain rice

Toast the pumpkin seeds in a dry non-stick frying pan. Bring the stock to the boil in a small saucepan, then keep warm. Peel the onion and garlic and chop finely. Sauté the onion and garlic in the oil until translucent. Add the rice, toast it briefly, while stirring constantly, and season with salt. Then add the wine and simmer until it has nearly evaporated. Add about 150 ml (5 fl oz) of the hot vegetable stock to the rice. Cook the rice for 35–40 minutes, stirring occasionally and gradually adding more stock. The rice is done when it is tender, but still has a slight firmness at the centre when you bite into a grain. While the rice is cooking, wash and trim the coiurgettes. Peel the carrot. Grate both vegetables. When the rice is done, stir the grated vegetables into it, season with salt and pepper, cover, and leave to stand for 5 minutes. Sprinkle the risotto with the pumpkin seeds and cheese.

Serves 2:

1 tbsp pumpkin seeds
400 ml (13 fl oz) vegetable stock
1 onion
1 small clove garlic
1 tbsp olive oil
150 g (6 oz) short-grain brown rice (healthfood shop)
Salt to taste
50 ml (2 fl oz) dry white wine
100 g (4 oz) courgettes
100 g (4 oz) carrot
Black pepper to taste
30 g (1 oz) Emmental, grated

Whole-Grain Rice

Fibre, like that found in whole-grain rice, rescues you from insulin weight gain. Enzymes in your intestines break down the starch of rice or grain into sugar molecules. The fibre from the grain hulls keeps the enzymes from doing this too quickly. As a result, sugar enters your bloodstream more slowly and triggers only a little of the fat-storing hormone insulin.

Power per serving:

484 calories

12 g protein • 18 g fat

65 g carbohydrate

power

Green Chick Pea Stir-Fry

Legumes provide lots of fat-burning protein

Wash the spinach well, remove the stems, and chop it coarsely. Cut the green pepper into quarters, remove the stem, ribs, and seeds, and wash and cut it into strips. Trim the spring onions, wash, and slice diagonally. Wash and trim the mange touts, removing any strings. Peel the ginger and garlic, and chop them finely. Heat the oil over a high heat in a wok and briefly sauté the ginger and garlic. Add the pepper strips, mange touts, and spring onions, and sauté for about 4 minutes, stirring constantly. Add the spinach, chick peas, and stock, and stir-fry for 2–3 minutes. Season to taste with salt, cayenne pepper, and lemon juice. Serve on plates with 1 tablespoon of yogurt in the centre of each serving.

Serves 2:

200 g (7 oz) spinach leaves
1 green pepper
150 g (6 oz) spring onions
100 g (4 oz) mange touts
1 small piece root ginger
1 clove garlic
1 tbsp corn oil
250 g (9 oz) tinned chick peas (drained)
3 tbsp vegetable stock
Salt to taste
Cayenne pepper to taste
1–2 tsp lemon juice
2 tbsp low-fat natural yogurt

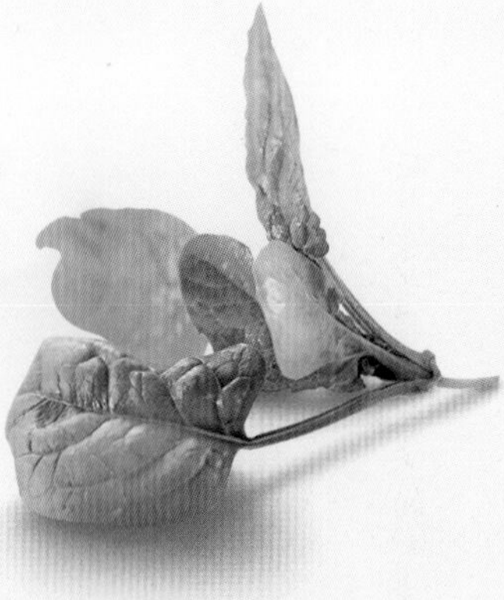

Guaranteed Vitamins

Select vegetables that are in season and grown locally. Always adhere to these basic principles: Buy fresh, use as soon as possible, don't cut up into pieces that are too small, don't soak too long, and cook gently. Follow the traffic light rule: one red, one green, and one yellow vegetable every day. This will guarantee a wide variety of vitamins and phytochemicals in your diet.

POWER PER SERVING:

492 CALORIES

42 G PROTEIN • 13 G FAT

82 G CARBOHYDRATE

power

Instant

Enjoy light pizza

Vegetable Pizza

For the dough, quickly knead together the yogurt, flour, baking powder, milk, 2 tablespoons of the oil, and 1/2 tsp salt. Preheat the oven to 200°C (400°F, Gas Mark 6). Grease and line a baking sheet. Roll out the dough to a thin rectangle on a lightly floured surface. Transfer it to the baking sheet and pierce the dough several times with a fork. Spread the tomatoes over the dough. Clean the mushrooms and cut into very thin slices. Trim the fennel, wash, cut it into quarters, and then into thin slices. Scatter the mushrooms and fennel over the tomatoes. Season the pizza with salt, and sprinkle with the chilli powder and cheese. Drizzle the remaining 1/2 tablespoon oil over the top. Bake the pizza for 25–30 minutes in the middle of the oven. Garnish with olives and basil, and serve.

Serves 2:

125 ml (4 fl oz) low-fat natural yogurt
150g (6 oz) wholemeal flour
1 tsp baking powder
3 tbsp low-fat milk
2 1/2 tbsp sunflower oil
Salt to taste
150 g (6 oz) chopped tinned tomatoes (drained)
75 g (3 oz) mushrooms
1 small bulb fennel
1 tsp chilli powder
50 g (2 oz) Gouda, grated
6 black olives (pitted)
6–8 fresh basil leaves

Chillis Spice up Your Life

Eat something spicy and your brain will be flooded with endorphins, the messenger chemicals that ease pain and lift your spirits. A good mood translates into a more active and slender you. Spiciness also heats up the fat cells, so they are more likely to move.

POWER PER SERVING:
545 CALORIES
23 G PROTEIN • 23 G FAT
64 G CARBOHYDRATE

power

Bean Sprouts and Chicken Stir-Fry

Wok cooking preserves nutrients

Cut the chicken breast into thin strips and season with pepper. Rinse and drain the bean sprouts. Remove the stem, ribs, and seeds from the pepper, and wash and cut it into strips. Trim the celery, wash, and cut it into thin slices. Peel the onion and dice it finely. In a small bowl, whisk together the chicken stock, soy sauce, sherry, and cornflour.

Heat 1 tablespoon of oil in a wok over a high heat. Stir fry the chicken for about 3 minutes, then remove it from the pan. In the remaining oil, stir fry the pepper, celery, and onion for 3 minutes. Add the sprouts and stir fry for 1 minute more.

Stir in the soy sauce mixture and cook until the sauce thickens, about 2 minutes. Add the chicken, briefly heat through, and season with pepper. Sprinkle with coriander and serve on a bed of rice.

Serves 2:

200 g (7 oz) boneless, skinless chicken breast
Black pepper to taste
200 g (7 oz) bean sprouts
1 red pepper
2 celery stalks
1 small onion
125 ml (4 fl oz) chicken stock
2 tbsp soy sauce
2 tbsp dry sherry
1 tsp cornflour
1 1/2 tbsp soya oil
2 tbsp chopped fresh coriander
Cooked brown rice

POWER PER SERVING: 315 CALORIES • 37 G PROTEIN • 8 G FAT • 19 G CARBOHYDRATE

Spinach Saltimbocca

A lighter version of a well loved classic

Wash the spinach well and remove the stems. Blanch the spinach in boiling, salted water for 1 minute, plunge it into cold water and drain. Squeeze the moisture out of the spinach and chop it coarsely. Season with salt, pepper, and nutmeg.

Serves 2:
300 g (10 oz) fresh spinach
Salt to taste
Black pepper to taste
Freshly grated nutmeg to taste
4 thin chicken breasts (about 50 g (2 oz) each)
1 tbsp olive oil
Juice of 1 lime
50 ml (2 fl oz) dry white wine
125 ml (4 fl oz) chicken stock
2 tsp cornflour
Cooked whole-wheat fettuccine

Place 1 tablespoon of the spinach on top of each chicken breast, fold them over, and fasten each one with a wooden skewer.

Heat the oil in a frying pan over a medium-high heat. Sauté the chicken pieces for 1–2 minutes on each side. Remove them from the pan, season with salt and pepper, and keep warm. Mix together the lime juice, wine, stock, and cornflour, and add it to the pan. Simmer over a low heat until the mixture thickens.

Season the sauce with salt and pepper. Add the chicken and the remaining spinach to the pan and simmer, covered, for 2–3 minutes. Serve with the fettucine.

White Meat

Meat is an important source of protein and iron, which makes it a fat burner. At the same time, however, beef, lamb, and pork contain a large amount of fat and purines. You should keep your consumption of red meat to a minimum. When you do indulge, choose the lower fat pieces from the fillet or tenderloin. Best of all, use white meat. Poultry and veal help you to go easy on bad fat.

Power per serving:
325 calories
30 g protein • 14 g fat
17 g carbohydrate

Sole with Spring Vegetables

Rich in iodine

Season the sole fillets with salt and pepper, and spread each with 1/2 tablespoon of the crème fraîche. Wash and shake the tarragon dry, then remove the leaves from the stems. Sprinkle some of the tarragon leaves over the sole fillets and roll them up tightly. Peel the kohlrabi and cut it into quarters. Peel the carrots. Cut both vegetables into thin slices. Trim and wash the mange touts. Peel and chop the onion.

Heat the oil in a saucepan over a medium heat. Add the onion and sauté until translucent. Add the kohlrabi, carrots, and mange touts, and sauté briefly. Pour in the stock, cover the pan, and simmer the vegetables for 5 minutes. Season the vegetables with salt and pepper. Stir in the remaining crème fraîche. Place the rolled sole fillets on top of the vegetables, cover, and simmer for 10 minutes over low heat. Chop the remaining tarragon and sprinkle on top. Serve with the rice

Serves 2:

4 sole fillets (about 50 g (2 oz) each)
Salt to taste
White pepper to taste
1 1/2 tbsp crème fraîche
1 sprig fresh tarragon
1 kohlrabi
200 g (7 oz) baby carrots
150 g (6 oz) mange touts
1 small onion
1 tbsp corn oil
150 ml (5 fl oz) vegetable stock
Cooked brown and wild rice

Fish, Please!

You should eat fish at least twice a week. It makes no difference what type – all fish is healthy. Salmon provides omega-3 fatty acids that prevent many chronic illnesses. Mackerel contains tyrosine, the material of fat-burning hormones. Fillet of sole is virtually fat-free.

POWER PER SERVING:

276 CALORIES

37 G PROTEIN • 13 G FAT

42 G CARBOHYDRATE

Stir-Fried Vegetables with Prawn

Melt away fat with fish protein

Trim and wash the mange touts. Blanch them in boiling, salted water for 1 minute, plunge them into cold water, and drain. Remove the stem, ribs, and seeds from the yellow pepper, and wash and cut it into strips. Peel the shallot and chop finely.

Serves 2:

150 g (6 oz) mange touts
Salt to taste
1 yellow pepper
1 shallot
1 tbsp corn oil
Pepper to taste
150 g (6 oz) raw peeled prawns
100 g (4 oz) cherry tomatoes
Handful of fresh dill
1 tbsp fresh lemon juice

Heat the oil in a frying pan over a medium heat. Add the mange touts, pepper, and shallot, and sauté for 5 minutes. Season with salt and pepper.

Add the prawns and sauté over low heat for 2 minutes. Cut the tomatoes in half and remove the stems. Wash the dill, shake dry, and chop. Add the tomato halves and dill to the pan and cook for 2 minutes more. Remove from the heat and toss with the lemon juice.

Midnight Snacks

Just before going to bed, raid the refrigerator one last time. For efficient fat burning you'll need protein and carbohydrates. Half a serving of yogurt with 2 tbsp of oat flakes stimulates the hormone serotonin for a peaceful sleep, as well as growth hormone, which breaks down fat and builds up muscle while you quietly slumber.

Power per serving:

161 calories

33 g protein • 5 g fat

43 g carbohydrate

power

Monkfish Ragout with Lentils

Fill up your tank with "super" fuel

Wash and peel the potatoes and carrot, then dice them. Trim the leek, slit it open lengthways, and wash and cut it into rings. Peel and dice the onion.

Serves 2:
150 g (6 oz) firm potatoes
1 carrot
1 small leek
1 small onion
2 tsp olive oil
250 ml (8 fl oz) vegetable stock
200 g (7 oz) cooked brown lentils
125 ml (4 fl oz) tomato passata
Salt to taste
Black pepper to taste
300 g (12 oz) monkfish fillet
2 tsp lemon juice
2 tbsp chopped fresh Italian parsley

Heat the oil in a large pan and sauté the onion until translucent. Add the potatoes, carrot, and leek, and sauté for 3 minutes. Pour in the stock, cover, and simmer for 10 minutes over low heat.

Add the lentils, passata, salt, and pepper. Simmer the mixture for 3 minutes more over medium heat.

Cut the fish into cubes, and season it with the lemon juice, salt, and pepper. Add the fish to the pan, cover, and simmer for 3–4 minutes over low heat. Season to taste with salt and pepper. Sprinkle the parsley over the top.

Olive Oil

Olive oil is the fountain of youth in Mediterranean countries. You too can cook with this precious tonic for a healthy heart and a slender figure. And don't skimp on the quality. Go for the purest and most natural "extra virgin" oil.

Power per serving:
565 calories
49 g protein • 9 g fat
70 g carbohydrate

power

Tuna Kebabs with Saffron Rice

Feast and stay thin

Peel the onion and dice it finely. Heat 1 tablespoon of the oil in a saucepan over medium heat and sauté the onion. Add the saffron and the rice, and sauté for 2 minutes. Pour in the wine and simmer. Add the stock, cover the pan, and cook for 40 minutes over low heat.

Cut the tuna into 2 cm (1 inch) cubes. Peel the onion and cut into 8 wedges. Remove the stem, ribs, and seeds from the pepper, and wash and cut it into pieces. Wash and trim the courgettes and cut into thick slices. Rinse and shake dry the sage. Thread pieces of fish, onion, pepper, courgette, and sage alternately onto wooden skewers. Peel and crush the garlic, and mix it in a shallow dish with the lemon juice, salt, and pepper. Coat the kebabs with the marinade, and set aside for about 30 minutes.

Heat the remaining 1 tablespoon of oil in a frying pan. Sauté the kebabs for 12–15 minutes, turning occasionally. Season the saffron rice with salt and pepper, and serve with the kebabs.

Serves 2:

1 small red onion
2 tbsp olive oil
2 pinches powdered saffron
150 g (6 oz) short-grain brown rice
60 ml (2 fl oz) dry white wine
300 ml (10 fl oz) vegetable stock
150 g (6 oz) tuna fillet
1 small white onion
1 small yellow pepper
100 g (4 oz) courgettes
8 fresh sage leaves
1 small clove garlic
1 tbsp lemon juice
Salt to taste
Black pepper to taste

power

Power per serving: 570 calories • 18 g protein • 25 g fat • 63 g carbohydrate

Index

Abbreviations
tsp = teaspoon
tbsp = tablespoon

First published in the UK by Gaia Books Ltd, 20 High St, Stroud, GL5 1AZ

Registered at 66 Charlotte Street London, W1T 4QE
Originally published under the title Fatburner Rezepte:

Translated in association with Silverback Books, Inc, US

Editorial: Katherine Pate
Nutritional Advisor: Lorna Rhodes

Printed in Thailand

ISBN: 1-85675 108 2
A catalogue record of this book is available in the British Library.

Caution
The techniques and recipes in this book are to be used at the reader's sole discretion and risk. Always consult a doctor before beginning a new eating plan or if in doubt about a medical condition.

Marion Grillparzer has a degree in food science and is a trained journalist. She lives in Munich and works as a freelance journalist; she has written for a number of magazines for many years. She is the author of numerous books focusing on nutrition and health.

Martina Kittler first studied food science and sports before turning her passion for cooking into a career. For almost eight years she worked as an editor for one of the largest German cooking magazines. Since 1991, she has been writing books and magazine articles as a freelance author. Her main subjects are modern, healthy nutrition and quick-and-easy everyday recipes.

Susie M. and **Pete Eising** have studios in Munich, Germany, and Kennebunkport, Maine. They both studied at the Professional Academy for Photodesign in Munich where, in 1991, they opened their own food photography studio.

For this book:
Photographic design:
Martina Görlach
Food styling:
Monika Schuster

Low Fat

Tasty meals for healthy eating
Friedrich Bohlmann
£5.99
ISBN 1 85675 113 9
Stay slim, healthy and full of vitality with quick and easy recipes to satisfy a healthy appetite.

Brain Food

Food to increase mental agility
Dr Ulrich Strunz
£5.99
ISBN 1 85675 197 X
Food to stimulate your brain. Increase your IQ, improve your memory and speed up your thought processes.

Fitness Food

Recipes to increase energy, stamina and endurance
Doris Muliar
£5.99
ISBN 1 85675 167 8
No more lethargy and exhaustion. Healthy food for power, conditioning and performance during exercise and afterwards.

Fitness Drinks

Juices and smoothies for energy and health
Dr Ulrich Strunz
£5.99
ISBN 1 85675 103 1
Delicious recipes for protein-packed power drinks rich in essential vitamins and minerals.

Energy Drinks

Power-packed juices: mixed, shaken or stirred
Friedrich Bohlmann
£5.99
ISBN 1 85675 140 6
Fresh juices packed full of goodness for vitality and health.

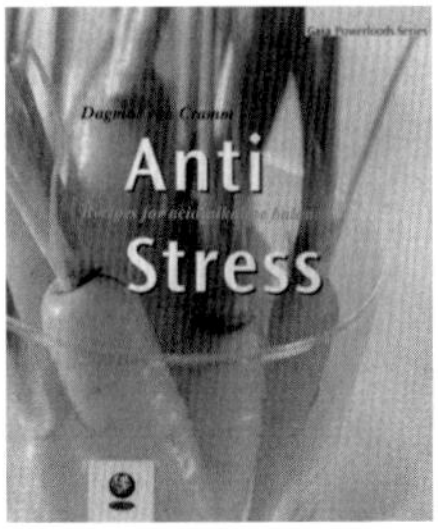

Anti Stress

Recipes for acid-alkaline balance
Dagmar von Cramm
£4.99
ISBN 1 85675 155 4
A balanced diet to reduce stress levels, maximise immunity and help you keep fit.

Detox

Foods to cleanse and purify from within
Angelika Ilies
£5.99
ISBN 1 85675 150 3
Detoxify your body as part of your daily routine by eating nutritional foods with cleansing properties.

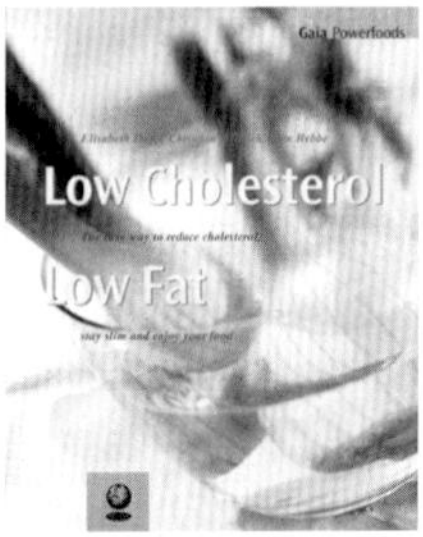

Low Cholesterol - Low Fat

The easy way to reduce cholesterol, stay slim and enjoy your food
Döpp, Willrich and Rebbe
£4.99
ISBN 1 85675 166 X
Stay fit, slim and healthy with easy-to-prepare gourmet feasts.

To order the books featured on this page call 01453 752985, fax 01453 752987 with your credit/debit card details, or send a cheque made payable to Gaia Books to Gaia Books Ltd., 20 High Street, Stroud, Glos., GL5 1AZ.
e-mail: gaiapub@dircon.co.uk or visit our website www.gaiabooks.co.uk